AF572184

make me aware lord

make me aware lord

DOROTHY K. GESCH

AUGSBURG PUBLISHING HOUSE
Minneapolis, Minnesota

MAKE ME AWARE LORD!

Library of Congress Catalog Card No. 75-135215

International Standard Book No. 0-8066-1102-2

Manufactured in the United States of America

dedication

To Roy,
who makes "love, honor, and obey"
a very real joy
and to our son, Gary,
who is constant proof of
answered prayer.

contents

preface

We can easily get so wrapped up and entangled in our daily demands and activities that soon we feel stifled and smothered. We live in our own little cocoon, which we helped spin. We feel secure and warm, perhaps, but still begin to want out, to struggle for new freedom, to have the larva emerge as a full grown butterfly, ready for new exciting ideas and new adventures.

Schedules and routines are followed each day, performed so mechanically and automatically that we seldom feel properly stimulated or mentally alert. We entertain only fleeting thoughts, and even our prayers become wooden and dull.

All too often God does not share a prominent place in our hearts as we go about the daily business of living. Christ is tucked away in a separate niche, while everyday life goes on without him—he who should share all our innermost thoughts, our joys as well as our problems.

The purpose of this book is to make us aware of more than blind routine; to make us more aware of others, the world we live in—common, ordinary things of our daily existence, and some more uncommon, but equally thought-stimulating. A new awareness can open new doors so we can enjoy a more meaningful life—really enjoy it, not just live it.

Some incidents or places that have occasioned these prayer thoughts may seem strange or foreign. But if you think about the places and happenings in your own life, you will see that you have the same opportunities to be directed to meditation and prayer. My hope is not that you will end up identifying with me, but that you will see yourself in God's picture.

Lord, make and keep me aware of all your blessings!

DOROTHY K. GESCH

make me aware lord!

Lord, this I ask.

Make me aware of
 the cry of one heart
 as well as
 the cries of the whole world.

Make me aware of
 the need to listen
 as well as
 the need to talk.

Make me aware of
 the people inside institution walls
 as well as
 the forbidding institution itself.

Make me aware of
 the need to love someone
 as well as
 the need of being loved.

Make me aware of
the awkward teenager
as well as
the cuddly baby.
Make me aware of
the strength we gain
from bearing burdens
as well as
the heaviness of the
burdens borne.
Make me aware of
the need for rain
as well as
sunshine.
Make me aware of
the source of infection
as well as
the infection itself.
Make me aware of
the quiet student who seeks
positive solutions
as well as
the blatant militant
who loudly voices
negative criticism.
Make me aware of
our promises to you
as well as
your promises to us.

it's morning, and i'm glad!

O Lord, this is the kind of a day
that ought to be put in the bank and saved.

Even the sun seemed anxious to rise!
The trees glisten with gems of dew
still poised and fresh.
The birds were never in finer voice
as their counterpoint melodies enrich the day.
And I never felt more alive.

It's morning, and I'm glad!

I feel a great awareness
of everything around me.

The jigsaw pieces of your creation
all fit together with perfection,
each complementing the other
in complete harmony.
How ingeniously you made it all!

I sense your nearness, loving Jesus.

There's a peace and joy
that transcends all—
just knowing you are with me.

I thank you so excitedly this morning—
for life,
for love,
for happiness,
for this beautiful world,
and the time to enjoy it.

give us this day

Why are we so obsessed, O Lord,
with where we want to go,
that we often fail to enjoy where we are?

We plan for tomorrow.
We overlook today.

Our lives come one day at a time.
It will never be any other way.
Yet how seldom we treasure
each day for what it is.
How seldom we live it to the "nth degree"!

You, heavenly father, give us a new day
with each arising of the sun,
a new chance for work, for relaxation,
for time with those who matter most to us.
Don't let us fritter away the days
in grasping and worrying
in the elusive hope
that our years to come
may be worry-free.

O Father, in these hectic times
we need to savor
every moment of every day.
One day at a time,
one step of our way,
with you alone, Christ,
giving us the power to live each step
as you would have us live it.

We regularly ask you
to "give us this day our daily bread,"
with all that it implies.
But now and then
wouldn't it be good
to ponder just the words,
  "Give us this day"?

ripples and reflections

Today the lake is a mirror,
reflecting images clearly.
It shows accurately and vividly
every detail around it,
its looking-glass surface
smooth and unruffled.

Yet at any time,
with very little to disturb it,
ripples begin to wave and dance,
distorting and twisting,
obscuring and clouding,
what had seemed so living, so real.

It is regrettable
what once was so perfect
now is so imperfect.
What once was clear image
now is only vague resemblance,
if, indeed, anything at all.

But I've learned to wait.
If nothing new descends to rile it,
it settles down once again
all glassy and polished,

duplicating the scene above
in all truth and beauty.

O Lord, there are days
when I can see you and my life
in amazing clarity.
Your love shows through
unmistakably, undistortedly.
Then suddenly the storms arise.

Calm the troubled waters of my life.
Smooth them with your love, O Christ.
Then as all becomes quiet
I can once again see your face
mirrored over my shoulder
smiling your benediction.

the ship in the bottle

The ship in the bottle
sits on the fireplace mantel.
It has to be dusted each week.

Poor ship!
Its sails are flying,
but it doesn't go anywhere.

Just a dustcatcher,
just an ornament,
reminding of what might be,
if the ship were not make-believe,
caught behind a bottleneck.

Lord, let me be
more than a dustcatcher.
Let me do what a child
of yours should do.

Don't let me contemplate
for too long a time
what might have been
- - - IF.

Keep me out of the land of make-believe.

I am in the here and now.
And you are too, Lord Jesus.
Let my actions prove that I am alive,
and that you live in me.

Let my ship sail free
into the wind.
Unhampered.

And as for bottlenecks—
let me never be one.

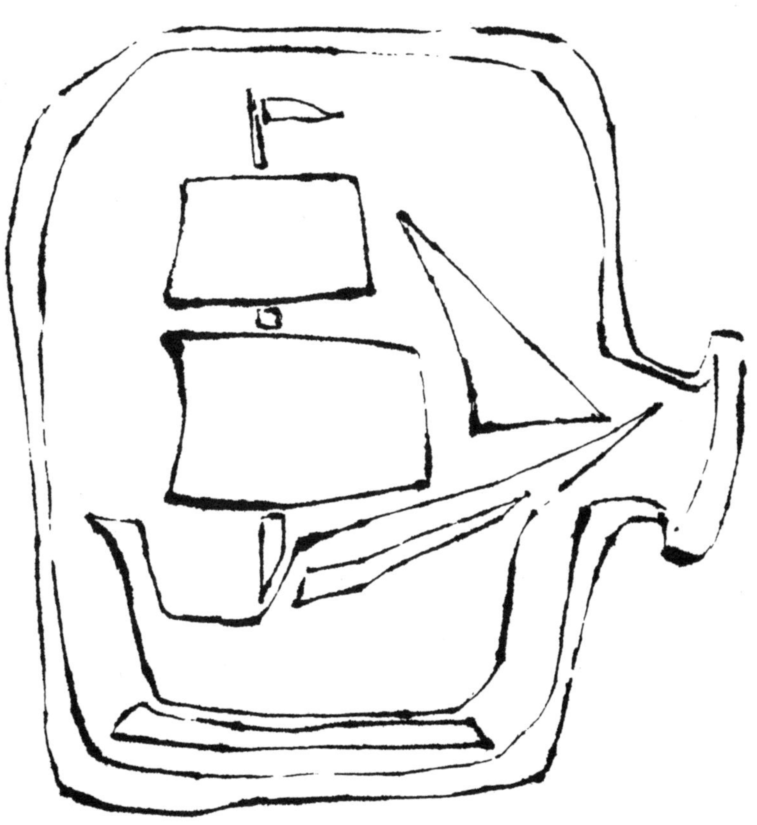

sometimes i feel like a child

Sometimes I feel like a child, Lord.
I find trouble in telling you
exactly how I feel.
I can't express it.
Words just don't come out right.

And yet you know what it is
I am really trying to say.
Fathers are that way.
You know what is deep in my heart,
even though I fumble in telling it.
I say one thing,
but mean another.
Maybe you even smile
at some of my illogical thoughts.
Sometimes I draw a complete blank.
I find myself empty of all thought
though I feel the real inner need
of talking to you.

Perhaps I don't want to face up to it.
A thought unexpressed can be more easily ignored.
Yes, maybe that's it.
Anyway, you know, Father, don't you?

And as my Father,
You know what is best for me.
You proved that
when you sent Jesus so long ago.

And as a child,
I need to be guided.
So lead me, Father.
Show me the way.
I need ask no more than that.

jesus' lamb

Was it purely by accident, Lord,
   or did you plan it to happen this way?

On this confused and mixed-up morning,
   as my hands were doing the routine things
      that always seem to need doing,
   there you were, on a prayer pamphlet cover,
      looking tenderly down
         at a wee white lamb
      which you cradled ever so gently
   in your strong, protective arms.
Concern and love is on your face
   as you clasp to your cloak
      the fortunate lamb.

"I am Jesus' little lamb - -"
   How the words of that childhood song
      come flooding back right now!
"For my Shepherd gently guides me,
   Knows my need, and well provides me - -"
We ask you for guidance,
   yet wonder how it will come.

This morning no sermon
  could be more eloquent
    than this one small picture!
I feel your presence,
  your power and love
    at a time I need
      to feel it so much.

As frantic, frenetic days race by,
  one as jumbled as the ones before,
    this painting seems heaven sent,
      from you to me,
    to make me aware once again
  of your constant love
    for all your children,
      even wondering, floundering me!

You "love me every day the same,
  even call me by my name."
That is a pretty personal thing, Lord.
  To think that you know my name!
And I ask, Lord Jesus, for a constant awareness
  so when things become harried and hectic
    I remember to take the time
      to call you by your name.

scrimshaw

O Lord of all of life,
even of dull monotony
and endless routines,
keep our spirits from drooping
by turning our eyes to all around us,
to that which we could enjoy
if we but try.

Your world is abounding
with beauty and meaning.
Let our boredom vanish
as we develop new interests
in the world
and the people
and the beauty around us.

I think of the old whalers
out of Nantucket and New Bedford,
who lived on the open sea
for years at a time,
one weary journey after another.

What constant monotony!
What unending boredom!
Yet out of that boredom was born
scrimshaw,
a new and delicate art
that has endured long
beyond the time of whaling ships.

The materials at hand
determined the art—
a whale's tooth or bone,
infinite knowledge
of sailing ships and churning seas,
and time—lots of time.

Hour after hour
they polished and etched.
Hulls and rigging
came to life on high waves.
As the design was black-inked
into the white shining ivory,
another moment of history became indelible.

O Lord of all life,
awaken me to the materials
and opportunities
with which you
have surrounded my life.

Let the beauty and meaning
you have placed into life
bring forth new beauty and meaning
in my life,
and from my life to others.

turned on

O Lord,
there are many things
in our homes today
that are useful
only when they are turned on—
a radio,
television set,
dozens of appliances,
even the light bulbs.
They serve no purpose
when the switch is off.

O Lord,
keep us aware
of the needs and hopes and desires
of our family, friends,
acquaintances, and strangers.
Don't let them ever feel
that our switch is turned off
and we are totally blind
to the problems of their lives.

O Lord,
send your Holy Spirit
to plug us in to you,
that your power
and your love
may course through us.

And keep our switch on
that our lives may always project
a picture of true worth and beauty,
with our whole being
vitally alive
and "turned on" to you
and the ones
whose lives we touch daily.

frayed nerves and tumbling walls

It's happening again today, Lord.
My nerves are playing tricks on me, tying me in knots. The churning stomach, the lump in the throat, the shaking hands, the tangled thoughts that just won't let go.

Things have a way of piling up, a little at a time. Not just one mountainous obstacle. Recurring small annoyances grate on the nerves, fraying the ends. It only takes a few added new ones to suddenly make life seem top-heavy. A tumble seems evident. This is when the walls come tumbling down.

I don't want my "walls" to tumble! I want to reinforce them with your own words of assurance. "Fear not, for I am with you. Be not dismayed, for I am your God." I need the calm that only you can give.

Give me the courage to erase my anxieties and fears by thinking them through prayerfully, then forgetting them.

You have told us, "Have no anxiety about anything, but in everything by prayer and supplication with thanksgiving let your requests be made known to God."

So I am asking you, dear Lord. Help me! Take away all my real or imagined problems. Grant me peace and contentment, a real release from tension.

Be with me always, Lord! I need you!

> "And the peace of God, which passes all understanding, will keep your hearts and your minds, in Christ Jesus."

the reject

She is an unknown, Lord Jesus.
A reject on the human slag pile.
Barely fifty years old. Yet a wreck.
Hollow eyes, a gaunt look, pasty skin.

As she puffs on her cigarette, lying here
in her hospital bed, the tattoo on her arm
is mute evidence of the kind of life she has led.

She says she has two sons, in their early twenties.
(She can't remember their ages exactly.)
They are both in the Navy—somewhere in this
world, but where in the world—only you know!

She lost her sons (her own words)
through cheap wine and a bad life.
Now she lies here alone, day after day,
young enough to live,
old enough not to care.

O Lord, you see how she listens
when a prayer is said for the woman in the next bed.

Her eyes closed, she is silent, her hands lie quiet.
"I have come to seek and to save that which was
lost." Those are your very own words.
How much more lost could one soul get?
Give her a new faith—first in you, above all,
then in herself, to start a fresh clean life
(if you will heal her abused body and soul).

Your power is at work.
The little grandmother in the next bed has shown
her trust in you. Today she requests an extra prayer
for her roommate, who is ready to hear of your love,
your forgiveness.
    You do love.
        You will forgive.
Give her the faith to believe this!

Christ Jesus, there are so many
such rejects, such unknowns in this world.
You only are their hope and salvation,
as you only are ours.
As you see them staggering and groping,
lift them in your strong arms
and guide them with your mighty hand.
Give them new life
and the ability to live it.

gray moods

My mood is gray today—a perfect match
to the weather outside my window.

Nothing black, nothing white,
only gray and shades of gray.

Routines are blindly followed. Dull, uninteresting, bland. Those words describe it perfectly. They even describe me perfectly today. I feel as dull as the dullest!

O Lord, give me the perking up that is needed. Show me how the simple things I must do each day, and every day, are serving their purposes in my life just as much as the big things, the interesting and exciting things. (And how many of those we really have, too!)

Do not let my gray moods rub off on those I love, dear Lord, mixing my grays with their sunny yellows and shiny reds to turn everything drab.

We each have our work to do. Let me do mine with joy, making me aware of the great blessings you have given me.

Constantly aware of your blessings—that's where the secret lies. If I can just remember you are with me, Jesus, that your love never fails, and that you offer me unending joy—somehow your brightness can break through into even the grayest of days.

Keep me cheerful and happy. "A merry heart maketh a cheerful countenance." So, dear Lord, change my heart from its feeling of boredom to a feeling of true happiness and love, which my smiling face can transmit to all around me.

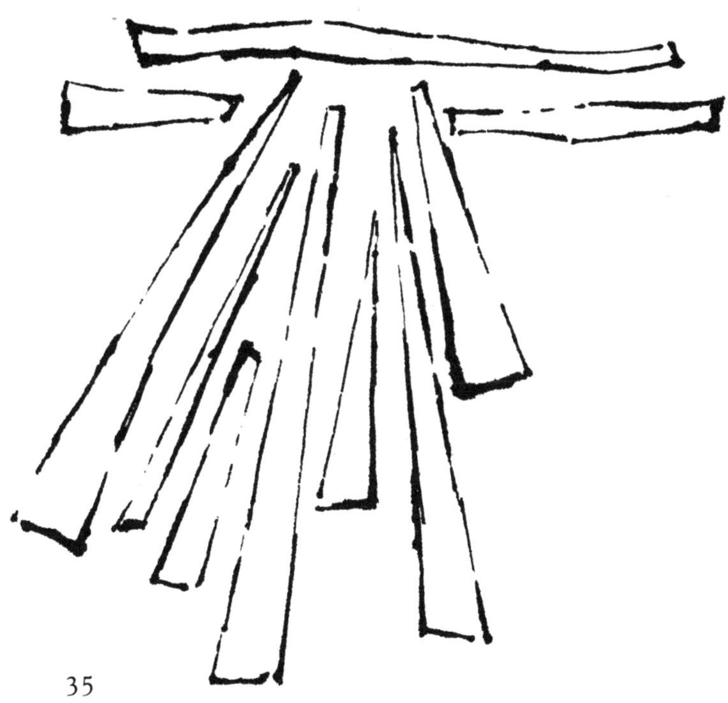

a shadow of a prayer

O Lord Christ, why am I so slow in telling you
what is in my heart and mind?

Why do I wait for preset moments
to bow my head, to fold my hands,
to assume a formal attitude of prayer?

Why, when thoughts, desires, hopes, anxieties,
constantly crowd my mind?
Shall these yearnings lie there neglected?
Shall they wither and die
(and a little of me too)
as they remain unexpressed and unattended?
Shall they be pushed into the shadows
just because I am waiting
for my preset time of prayer?

Peter's unplanned, "Lord, save me!"—
a blind man's, "Have mercy on me!"—
my own sigh of thanks
as brakes bring a car to a screeching halt—
could there be more perfect prayers?

A few right words at the right time,
a simple thought directed straight to you
in sincere and fullest faith—
do they not mean more than proper sentences
at proper times?

Dearest Jesus, you assured
that you are with us always.
Keep us aware of your presence and nearness
that we—
in thought and prayer—
may always be with you.

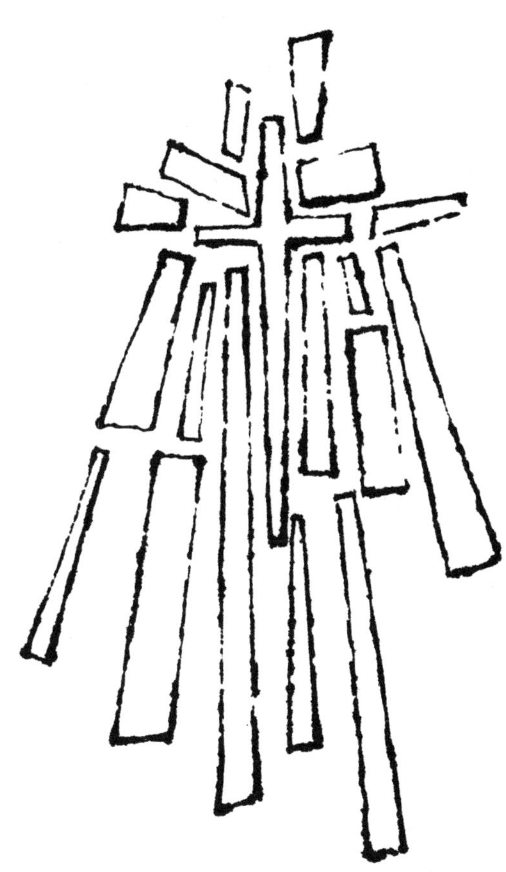

night blindness

O Lord,
thank you for putting little red danger signals
along life's roadway.
Perils of many kind await us,
many because of our own foolishness,
our own shortsightedness,
our own "night blindness."

A night walk along trails
in the Florida Everglades
shows tiny brilliant red lights
shining through the darkness,
down among the mangroves.

Spotlight those red flashes of light.
They are eyes—alligator eyes!
Eyes that shine in the night—
no danger in themselves,
but real warnings of immediate danger.
Step no further!
Danger lurks ahead!

Heavenly Father,
let your warning signals
keep me from straying
off the safe path
that you have laid out for me.

Give me perceptive eyes
with Christ the perfect lens
to correct my "night blindness."
Keep my senses alert.
Keep my vision unclouded.
Let me see danger and temptation
for what they really are!

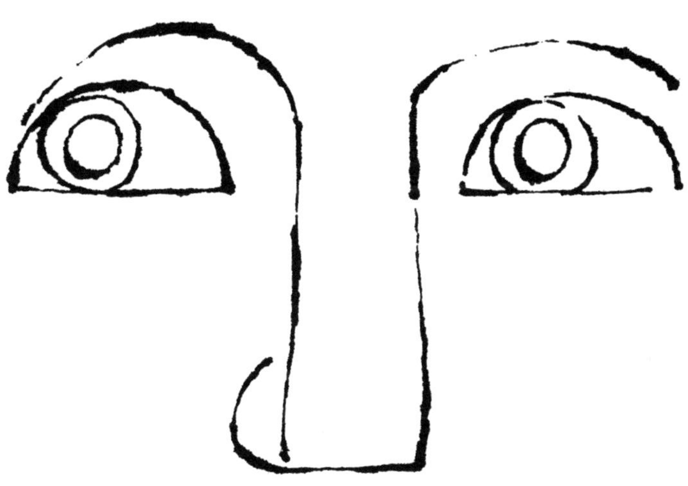

man's forgotten children

Man's forgotten children.
Mixed-race children,
half oriental, half occidental,
not theirs, not ours.
Belonging to no one,
belonging to everyone.
Children of the world,
if the world will have them.

Forgotten and abandoned,
mistreated and abused,
starved for food,
starved for love.

O Lord of all,
bless mightily those people
who have that extra measure of love
to include another little face
in their family circle,
with no thought of
what they are doing,
or of being noble,

but just one of thankfulness
that you have given
this precious little one
to them
for their very own.

What was it you said, Lord Jesus?
"He who receives
one such little child
in my name,
receives me?"

Christ, give us a love
like yours
for yours—
all of yours.
May we see
man's forgotten children
as God's unforgettable children.

at time of accident

Dear Father in heaven,
my heart overflows with thanks to you
for keeping my dear husband safe in your care,
in his hour of utmost danger and ultimate accident.
We could so easily have lost him
from our home and life.

You with your eternal love provided everything we need so broken bodies can eventually mend,
and life can proceed as before.

Bless mightily, dear Father, the doctors, technicians, nurses, and all those in medical science
who contribute their knowledge and help
when we need it so desperately.
(As well as the encouragement and cheer they give to us who fret and worry about our loved ones.)

Keep us from undue anxiety,
for we know you will work out all things for good.

Keep us firm in our love to you—
you who loved us all so much
that you let your own son suffer pain and death
to save us eternally.
"He helps us free from every need
that hath us now o'ertaken."

To say thank you, dear Father, is so inadequate,
but it is with very grateful hearts that we do
say it now.

Thank you so much.

the wind at our backs

O Lord, some days can be downright disagreeable!
The winds are harsh and cruel.
They bite and numb the face.
Yet, summer sun or winter wind,
life must go on at its accustomed pace.
With head lowered and shoulders hunched,
we fight the wind and trudge ahead.

Suddenly the windy gusts change course.
Though just as forceful as before,
now they are blowing at our backs,
pushing us forward, lightening our load,
making us seem mere featherweights.
What once was hindrance is now help.

Lord, be with us through the winds and storms
that buffet us along life's way.
And let us not be filled with fear.
You, who could command, "Peace! Be still!"
can bring quiet to our restless hearts.
You can calm the raging storm.
You could, Lord Jesus!
But is that the answer to our prayer?

You know when we can stand no more,
    when feet are staggering,
    when minds are faltering.
Perhaps your love sees fit
    to let the winds blow on.
Then let them blow!

But not at our faces, Lord,
    upsetting, deterring us,
        blowing us off course.
    Let the wind be at our backs
        to push us gently forward.

no lasting commitments?

There has been a rash of advertising lately for items made of disposable materials.

Now you can have dresses, flowers, napkins, bedspreads, sheets, and pillowcases— all made of paper.

A popular magazine commented that these are very sharp items, ideal for the impulse buyer, since they are bought with no eye to the future, where there is no kind of lasting commitment with the purchase.

Lord, I think that's one of our biggest troubles today! We are so hesitant to make any kind of lasting commitment, in anything.

Why are we so overly cautious about long-range investing in what is worthwhile? Shouldn't we look for lasting values— something that can endure over the years? Dare we be interested in the "now" and not the "later"? Why do we look on commitments of any kind as being too confining?

You made commitments to us, Lord. Your whole Word is full of promises. Some you've already kept. Others you still intend to keep.

Christ himself was a commitment you made to us. So was the giving of his life. So is the crown of life you promise through him.

Lord, don't let us be afraid to make lasting commitments to you—or to each other.

the door

O Lord,
what is happening?
Am I imagining it,
or are you opening a door,
just a crack,
to show you really heard
my questioning call?

I didn't even know
what to ask for.
I only asked to be shown the way.
Are you showing me something now,
 already—so soon?

The light is beginning to creep
in through that door ajar.
Not enough to show the plan,
just enough to show
that the door isn't locked.

O Lord, let a breath of fresh air
come blowing through that door,

dissipating all the stuffiness
  and staleness
that has been accumulating
for so long.
Breathe life into this deadness.

Thank you, Lord.
You heard.
You knew the solution all along.
(And now I know there is one.)

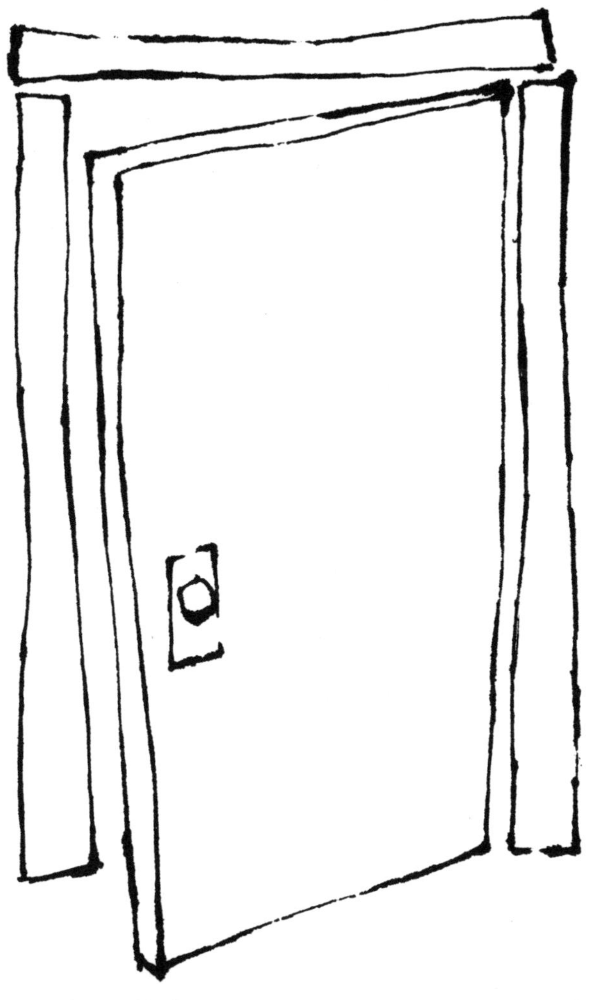

"surely the lord is in this place!"

O Lord, amid the rush of city life
I sit a moment, thinking of the day
we stood atop the jagged cliffs
of Monhegan Island,
hours distant from Maine's rockbound coast.

Already as the little supply and mailboat
tooted its way to the wharf,
we knew this had to be
one of the world's true beauty spots.

Our hearts wanted to sing out,
"All things bright and beautiful,
the Lord God made them all."

The insistent breeze carried a tang,
a blend of pine and sea.
The slight sprinkling of houses
huddling together on the leeward side
allowed the rest of the island,
as far as eye could see,
to remain just the way you created it, Lord.

No streets, no cars, a few scant miles of land,
a handful of people,
far outnumbered by resident seagulls.

In the gray predawn we walked,
as do the island folk,
upon that wooded land
to clifftop perch above the crashing surf—
to sit in silence, as they do,
and marvel at the awesome splendor
of the slowly rising sun.
We felt you very close to us, Lord.
The island seemed a Spirit-filled cathedral.

Yet, at our side, a one-day visitor
pulling her sweater tightly about her,
tossing her head defiantly,
jarred the silence with
"This just has to be
the most godforsaken place
in the entire world!"

O God, this is your world!
It shows throughout
the marks of your glory
and love.

Keep us ever aware
of your presence—
in the quiet spectacle of nature,
in the disturbing congestion of crowds.
"The Lord, thy God, is with thee,
whithersoever thou goest."
Let us never forget it.

the mark of a good listener

Having a ready heart for others
may also mean having a ready ear.

Who knows that better than you, my heavenly
Father!
How many trivial things we babble on about
endlessly
to you. But how lost we would be without that
opportunity!

It is so good to talk things over with someone—to communicate our needs to others. Problems brought out into the open often vanish into thin air.

I know that being able to talk to someone, dream to dream, heart to heart, even though no solution can be reached, is some of the best therapy in the world.

Father, let me become a ready ear for others. Let me be genuinely enthusiastic over their happiness. Let them bubble on about it to me, knowing I share their joy.

And if there is some way I can be of help, let me be the help I should!

Joys need sharing,
problems baring,
someone caring.

Make me like Jesus—to lend an ear, to reach a hand at the faintest cry. Let the love of Christ allow me to hear others, and show love to them, in his name.

If I can venture any advice, let me give it as a true friend. If the problem is beyond my capabilities, let me be just as attentive as their vague, agonized thoughts are turned into words.

Your own words can soothe and calm the best. Let me remember them, and share them with others.

"Weeping may endure for a night,
but joy cometh in the morning."

for food

I just got home from a trip to the supermarket.
Thanks are long overdue, Lord, for the wonderful
variety of food at our fingertips.

You have favored our country so richly
  with an oversupply of everything,
    including our food.
Keep me always grateful
  that you have given us so much!

How often I see turned up noses
  at food on the table.
I think of the wise words in Proverbs:
  "The full soul loatheth an honeycomb;
   but to the hungry soul
   every bitter thing is sweet."

We, with our plenty,
  are finicky and difficult to please,
    while some poor deserted child
      must grub away hungrily
    in a garbage dump

like a little animal,
intent on nothing but survival.

I thank you, Lord, that I do not have to claw my way through the garbage cans of this world to stay alive. But I pray for those who do.
Relieve their suffering and gnawing hunger,
through me and through others around the world.

Use me in placing food and life
into their reaching hands.
What was it Jesus said?
"I was hungry
and you gave me no food?"
"Inasmuch as you did it not
to one of the least of these,
you did it not to me?"

O Lord, I can't feed all your hungry children.
But let my love do something.

i am afraid

It is night, Lord. (And it is so dark.)
And I am all alone. (So very alone!)
And the house is so big. (It never seemed bigger.)
And I hear little noises. (So many of them.)

I am afraid!

Was it the house that creaked? (Or a twig that snapped?)
Is the sound outside? (Or somewhere inside?)

Oh, why am I so foolish?

Turn on some music. (That will drown out my all too vivid imagination.)
Turn on more lights. (Who am I fooling?)

Calm my uneasiness, Lord!

Take away all my unfounded fears. (And the pounding heartbeat and icy fingers.)

Quiet me with your Word.

"Fear not, for I am with Thee." (Oh, be with me, Lord!)
"When I am afraid,
I put my trust in thee." (Give me such trust!)

And so Lord, let me sleep,
a sweet, untroubled sleep,
"for thou, Lord, only
  makest me dwell in safety."

"Lord Jesus, who dost love me
O spread thy wings above me
And shield me from alarm.
Though Satan would devour me
Let angel guards sing over me,
'This child of God shall meet no harm.' "

the God's eye view

The silver jet climbs higher in the heavens.
Man-created ugliness is cloaked by God-created beauty.

The sea is vividly colored, with a froth of lace at its neckline. Oil slicks and refuse are obscured.

Houses are scaled to miniature size, each almost identical to the one beside it.

Cars seem propelled in all directions at once, one crawling to where the other has already been.

In minutes the large city is left behind. Man's inventiveness, with chimneys belching out their smoke and foul smells and choking smog is gone.

Your world, Lord, is shiny and clean, sparkling like a new toy. The countryside stretches ahead, so large, so inviting, while the fluff of clouds softens the landscape like some big gift-package bow.

Hovering midair all life seems to hang in the balance. Even the powerful jet seems to throb and bobble, dangling from some unseen wire of dubious strength. Only your world seems enduring and eternal.

Mountains stand like papier-mache relief work on a map, small and unimposing, yet grand in shape and jewelled peaks.

O Lord, your God's eye view of us must make you sad.
How many stains and blots we have put on your most exquisite landscape.

You have blessed us with the genius of discovery and inventions. Our lives have been enriched by it. Now make us willing, and show us how to undo the ugly scars that are the by-product of our work.

As small as man looks from your view, it is remarkable that you bother with him at all! Yet we know not even a sparrow falls to the ground but that you know it. Not one person lies outside the scope of Christ's love.

Watch over our human race! Don't let us invent ourselves right off the face of the earth!

You made perfection. Cover our imperfection!

"the lord watch between me and thee"

Oh how I pray, Lord,
that you will hold your hand of protection
over my husband,
as he spends these days away from home.

I watched his plane climb heavenward
(while I felt quite earthbound.)
I saw it become a small glint of silver,
then totally vanish into thin air,
with only a vapor trail as evidence.

The sudden separation of it all hit me.
You know, Lord, that I hesitated a moment,
then breathed a phrase,
a beautiful prayer in itself,
that has been especially meaningful,
warm and comforting,
to us over the years.

"The Lord watch between me and thee,
when we are absent one from another."

That says it all for now,
doesn't it, Lord?
All our cares and concerns for each other
are covered in that one plea.
If you are with us
what could harm us?
If Christ's love worked our eternal good,
could it fail us now?

I also thank you for letting me feel lonely now.
(Too many wives couldn't care less.)
I thank you that it is only miles
that separate us.
(Too many husbands and wives
never experience a real togetherness.)

So at this bittersweet time of separation
I know we both
are holding this one thought,
"The Lord watch between me and thee,
when we are absent one from another."

our masks are showing

Life is not a masquerade, heavenly Father.
But our masks are showing.

So often our expressions are fixed, noncommittal.
Nod.
  Smile.
    Frown.
      All at the proper moment.

Accept the accepted.
  Reject the rejected.
    Take the easy way.
  That's the way of our day, isn't it, Lord?
We are so afraid of wearing our hearts on our sleeves
  that sometimes we can not find them at all.

Don't be yourself. Adjust the mask.
  Don't let your true feelings show.
    Approval of the masses.
      Is this what we really want?

O Lord, what hypocrisy, sham, and make-believe
  there is!

Let me be myself, Father.
Let others be themselves.
Let us take a stand,
if there is a stand that needs taking.
Let our faces mirror our feelings genuinely.
Let Christ show through as the very realness
of our real and truthful lives.

O Father, if my opinion differs with others
let me disagree, yet not be disagreeable.

And when my face is smiling,
let it match my heart!

my question mark

O Lord, I am looking for answers.

You know the questions.
I don't have to voice them.

I am mixed-up.
I don't know what I want.
I could jump from bad to worse.

Show me the way.
If my ideas are logical,
give them substance
and help them work out.

If not, let me accept
the way things are,
knowing this is the better way.

"Seek and ye shall find,"
You promised, Lord Jesus—
You, who are both way and truth.

Give me faith that knows
You not only have the answers—
You are the answer.

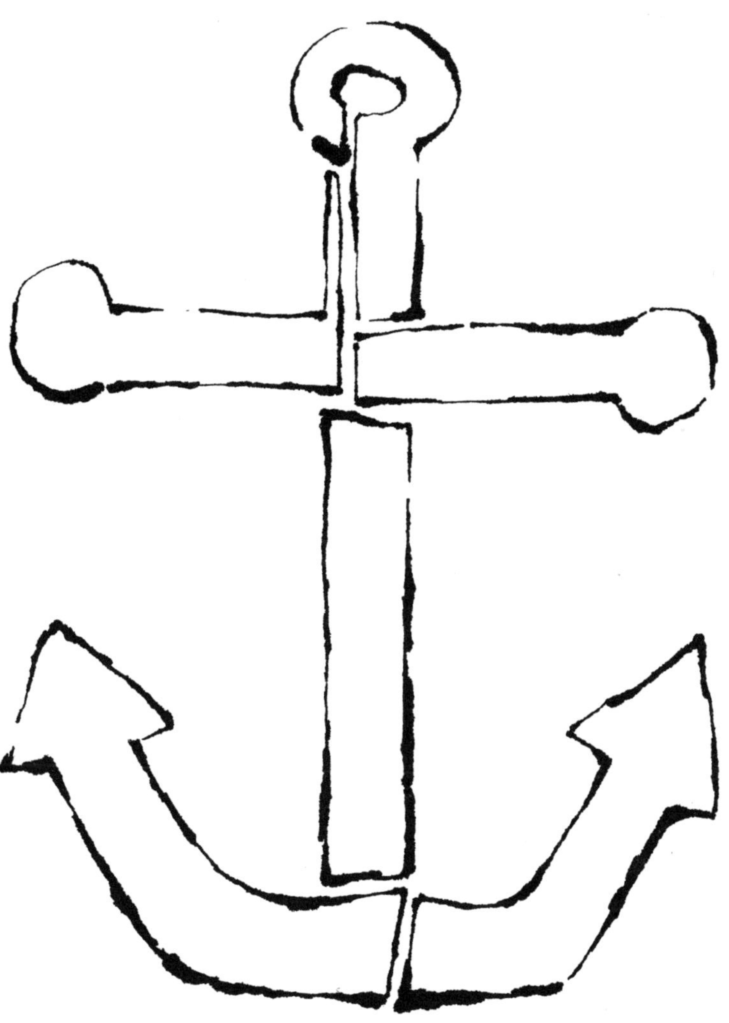

consistent living

Flowers blossom in brilliant profusion in their beribboned containers at the florist's shop.

What extraordinary beauty! Will they continue to bloom this way?

The gardener says "No." He says they are cultivated to produce the heavy mass of bloom all at once. It is really only a one time showpiece. Then if it does not die it quickly loses its vitality. Its strength is gone.

O God, you have created flowers to blossom in riots of color, up mountainsides, in verdant meadows and valleys. Year after year they clothe the soil with breathtaking beauty. Each wilting bloom gives promise of more to come.

We have succeeded in using built-in beauty for a momentary show, a one-time stand. Yet in so doing we have produced something that is almost dead before it really lives. And in such beauty of today, there is no promise for tomorrow.

Lord Jesus, don't let us do that to our lives. Show us how important it is to live constantly, to be strong through the years, to show what we are, and whose we are all the time.

May we not have one sudden spurt of faith in you, which then wilts and withers and dies. Our beauty and strength is ever in you, our Lord. Come what may, keep our faith strong and in full bloom constantly and consistently.

the human touch

How cold, how antiseptic it sounds—
"Untouched by human hands."

In this day of computers,
of a mechanically programmed world,
we need to know the warmth and tenderness
of the individual, human touch—
of a hand extended
to our own groping one.

I need it, dearest Jesus.
I dread to think
how alone and helpless I'd be
if I did not feel your nail-torn hand
holding tightly on to mine,
keeping me ever at your side.

I thrill to other hands I hold,
thanking for the love I know
because our lives have come together.

O Lord, let me also be the human touch
for others.

Let me not coldly put my signature
on a predigested, printed message
when my hand can add words
that show I understand and care.

Keep my hands from becoming so calloused
by much use and abuse
that they prove to be insensitive
to the miseries, the hurts,
the feelings of inadequacy
of those around me.

Make them strong
as well as compassionate,
that I may lend my strength,
my faith in you,
to one who is staggering
alone and friendless.

love affair with the mountains

I'm convinced, Lord, that if more people had a little hideaway house in the brisk, clean, pine-scented air in the mountains, there would be fewer breakdowns.

All is tranquil—peace itself. No traffic. No maddening rush. Neighbors act as neighbors should—friendly, warm, interested, and interesting. The love of the outdoors, of the beauties of your creation seem to bind all people together in a mutual bond.

The rugged strength of the mountain peaks, the blue-green coolness of the nestled-in lakes, the pine trees snuggling everything down in one big feel of solitude and contentment—all assert that this spot is placid and beautiful.

When life comes crashing down on our ears, how pleasant it is to retreat to the hills "from whence cometh our help."

When the hurry of the "downstairs world" is left far below, a walk through the forest can give time to think, to see things more clearly, to gain a whole new perspective.

Summer or winter—its soothing effect on tense, tired minds is a balm you must have created for just such ills.

The snows of winter insulate and isolate.
The heralds of spring, the snow flowers, poke their red heads through the hard, barren ground.
The wild iris climb the hillsides,
crowning them with purple.
Baby violets, flowering dogwood.
And always the birds and squirrels,
chipmunks and deer.
It is another world.
Yours.

How can we help but thank you for giving us
such a large piece of heaven right here on earth,
so close to our daily workaday world!

You must love the mountains.
You made them so beautiful!

in his father's footsteps

Heavenly Father, one day I watched
a man striding along the beach.
   A little boy tagged along behind
      hopping from one footprint to the other.
He didn't always make it.
   His legs were too short.
But, oh, how he tried
   to follow in his father's footsteps.

Heavenly Father, I try too!
   You left a path for us to follow,
      clearly marked, clearly defined.
I know we should follow in your footsteps.
   But sometimes the steps seem too big
      for us to reach.
   Sometimes they seem to be washed away
      leaving us in doubt as to our direction.

Yet, if we look closely,
   the path is unmistakably there.
All we must do is learn to follow,
   difficult though it may seem at times.

Lead us, Father, in the path of Christ.
I see him as your son
  whose footsteps perfectly match yours.
But they are man-sized steps,
  and his hand is there to help us.

Lead us, Father, where you would have us go,
always close enough that we do not lose sight of you,
always far enough ahead to set the course and pace.

for those who are sick

It is staggering, Lord, to think of all the sickness and misery in the world. Hospitals, convalescent homes, and other institutions are filled to overflowing. Thousands of other incurables remain quite unnoticed and alone in their own apartments or houses.

So much of this atmosphere becomes very depressing, Lord. It seems almost a miracle to be untouched by illness. Why should we be spared more than others? Or is a sword hanging over our heads, ready to fall at any minute?

Take away these morbid thoughts, Lord Jesus. Replace them with thanks for all your kindnesses and mercies.

I pray for those, wherever they may be, who are at this moment ill and discouraged, broken in body or mind. Heal, Lord Jesus, where it is your will to heal. Bring peace and comfort where there is to be no healing.

I pray in faith, knowing that you who could and did dispel illness, handicap, and even death, can do so just as surely now. Yours is the power and the love.

Be with the families of those lying sick and weakened. It is difficult for them also, to see the ones they love laid low by suffering. Give them a large measure of courage, and let it be contagious, spreading its hope and cheer to those distressed.

Take away self-pity, which causes nothing but heartache and loosens the grip on reality. Sagging shoulders and drooping spirits invite despair to make its home within. Give all those ill ones the knowledge that, by your grace, this too shall pass.

Where there is trembling and fear, renew faith and trust in you, Lord Jesus, as well as strength. Show how much cause there is for real joy, and let it truly be believed!

the dovekie

O God of all nature, the great, the small,
the magnificent, the insignificant,
keep our eyes wide open
and our whole beings aware
of what we can learn
from the simplest of things.

The dovekie, a rather strange bird,
may be seen on Cape Cod beaches
after stormy winds have blown it in,
leaving it helpless and stranded.

And there it sits—an easy prey—
since this odd little bird
cannot walk on land,
nor even take off in flight from it.
He is held captive by himself.

If no one finds him there,
landlocked and marooned,
and slips him gently
back into the water,

he must sit and wait
for the oncoming tide
to sweep the sand
and float him seaward once more,
from where he can take to the air,
to safety and security.

O Lord, though we may not like to admit it,
aren't we like the dovekie?
A storm may come, a storm may go.
And there we sit, stranded and helpless,
easy victims to many dangers,
because we haven't learned to walk,
let alone fly,
captives of our own
inabilities and inhibitions.

Lord Jesus Christ, it is in times like these
that we see how dependent we are on you—
on your strong and capable arms.
Lift us up, and carry us to safety.

Then when we are once again secure in you,
we can fly and soar to new heights
far above the troubles and disappointments
that threatened to hold us back.

"I can do all things through Christ
who strengthens me."
But without you, I can do nothing.
Keep me ever mindful of this,
when storm clouds threaten
to drive me away from you, Lord Jesus.

make us real

Dear Lord, I heard
a successful man reminiscing with his wife.
They spoke of days long gone,
   days filled with charm and treasure.

Today's good fortune was sweet,
   but yesterday's struggle had its sweetness too.

One thing he said keeps haunting me.
It seems the key to long-locked secrets:
   "We were real then."

It has been hard—
   meager income, big expenses,
      no furs, no luxuries.
   But also no pretense, no sham,
      no image to uphold.
   Just the genuine article,
      the real thing—
      two people being themselves.

Lord, make and keep us real.
It is not what we have that really matters,

but what we are—
and what we mean to each other.

We will enjoy our successes and gains,
and all else your love provides.
And we are confident that your love
that sent Jesus to bring
the peace of forgiveness
and joy of eternal life
into our lives,
will always bless us with all we need.

Just don't let things change us.
Keep us real people.
Let our house always be a real home
where the glow and warmth of firelight
reflects the love and contentment
on the faces of those within.

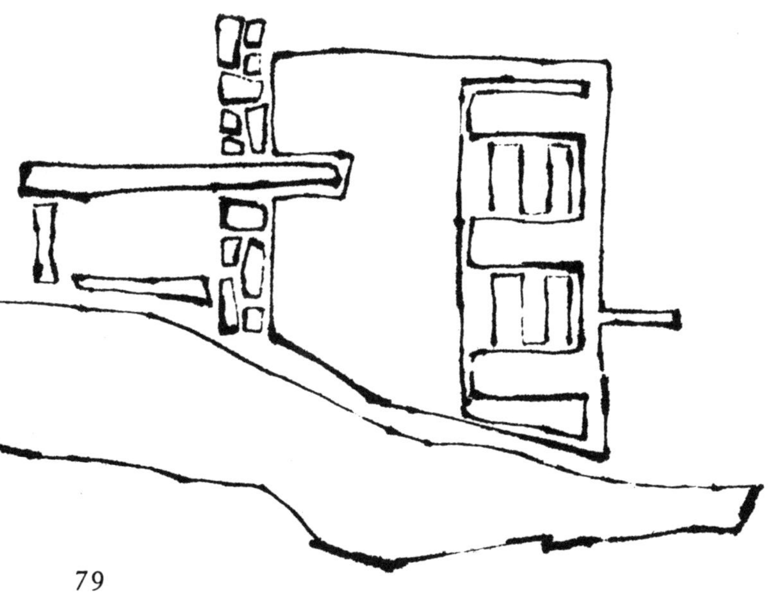

thoughts on a sunday morning

Dear Lord, it isn't often on a Sunday morning
that things are all done early.
Routines gobble up time quickly—
beds to make, breakfast to cook, dishes to wash,
time to dress and get ready for church.

We don't often have the time
to stop and think for a few minutes
about where we are going,
or even the "why" of it.

Every day of the week has its normal routines.
We can go through them with our eyes closed.
Sunday is no exception.
But let us never lose the joy
(that is all too easily forgotten)
of our Sunday morning routine.

Time with you should never be considered routine.
It should be contemplated.
We should go to your house
in the proper frame of mind,

and for the right reasons.
It should never be to keep up an image,
or to see friends we will not see until next Sunday.
It is only to see you,
who are with us every day of the week,
every day of our lives.
It is to have the light of Christ,
our precious Lord and Savior
shine into our hearts
more beautifully through your Word
than through the most magnificent stained glass window.
We go to your house to learn and listen and worship,
and then to once again go,
but to take you with us, back to our homes.

Let the distractions in the church that inevitably come
not distract us from our worship of you.
Give us food for thought and action
that will lead us through another week
with its humdrum and sameness.
Let the music inspire
and the spoken Word
fall on ready hearts and ears.
Show us that this is truly your house,
and the place where honor dwells.

road slippery when flowers fall

Father, I dream of a life filled with nothing but obvious blessing. How often I pray that all may be smooth and abundant and beautiful. But should I?

I think of a sign posted along some roadways in Japan. It warns:
"Road Slippery When Flowers Fall."

Graceful cherry trees border these lanes. When their pink petals start falling, it is a scene of indescribable beauty, like drifts of pink snow.

But this delicate blanket hides a treacherous road—rutted and corrugated. Yet, it is not of this that the sign warns. Not of the hidden dangers, but of the flowers themselves. But can it be? Cherry blossoms a potential trouble?

Should a sudden stop be necessary, a car can easily skid out of control, as if on icy pavement.

Father, keep us grateful for the flowers, the beautiful blessings, in our lives. We have so many of them! But do not let them make our life slippery, so we slide into easy temptation. Keep us from becoming drugged by the soft fragrant sweetness of our flower-filled days, lest we become oblivious to danger ahead.

Father, make us doubly thankful that you have richly showered us with other blessings, that are pure and unfading. There's no deception in the beauty of our Savior's love. There's no danger of being lulled into a sense of false security. The beauteous hope and peace he gives are real, and always will be real.

And yet, Father, I know I shall also continue to pray for blossoms, to brighten the drabness and soften the harshness in our days. I see this also as your love.

vacation—getaway time

At last it has come, Lord!
   Vacation time! Getaway day.
I can scarcely believe it.
   The months of planning, saving, and waiting
      are over.

Suitcases bulge,
   the car is loaded,
      roadmaps clearly marked
   are already dog-earred and creased.

But, dearest Jesus, before we leave we pause
   to ask your guidance and protection.
The way is new,
   the road is long,
      and destinations far distant.

How good it is to leave the old ruts
   for at least a few weeks.
So good to laugh again,
   to reknit family ties.

I know you once said,
"Come away by yourselves
to a lonely place,
and rest a while."

Give us a light heart, Lord,
so our holiday is carefree and relaxed.
But keep us mindful it is you, Christ Jesus,
who gives us all these pleasures,
and every happy time in life.

Keep your protecting arm around us,
so that at vacation's end
we will arrive home refreshed,
invigorated, uplifted, and safe
in body and soul.

a diamond in the rough?

Father, how often do we not try to excuse a person's bad behavior?
We say he is really a diamond in the rough—would give you the shirt off his back if it came to a showdown.

Diamond in the rough? Perhaps. Who knows for sure? But no diamond in the rough has the value of the finely cut gem in the jeweler's display case.

Only after painstaking work at an expert's hands does the stone show its true brilliance and sparkle.

Flaws in a diamond do not make it a diamond in the rough. They may make it quite worthless.
A discard.

Is bad behavior, or a loud mouth, or vulgar talk ever justified? Are they marks of a diamond in the rough? Or are they flaws?

Don't let me be content to be a diamond in the rough, Father. Work me over in whatever way you see fit.

Once you sent Jesus as the perfect gem. Now, with your expert hands, develop me to resemble him, at least to a degree.

Use little problems as well as big crises to chisel smooth facets in my rough exterior, that I may catch and reflect your brilliant light—that I too may be a priceless gem, with true sparkle shining through my life into the lives of those around me.

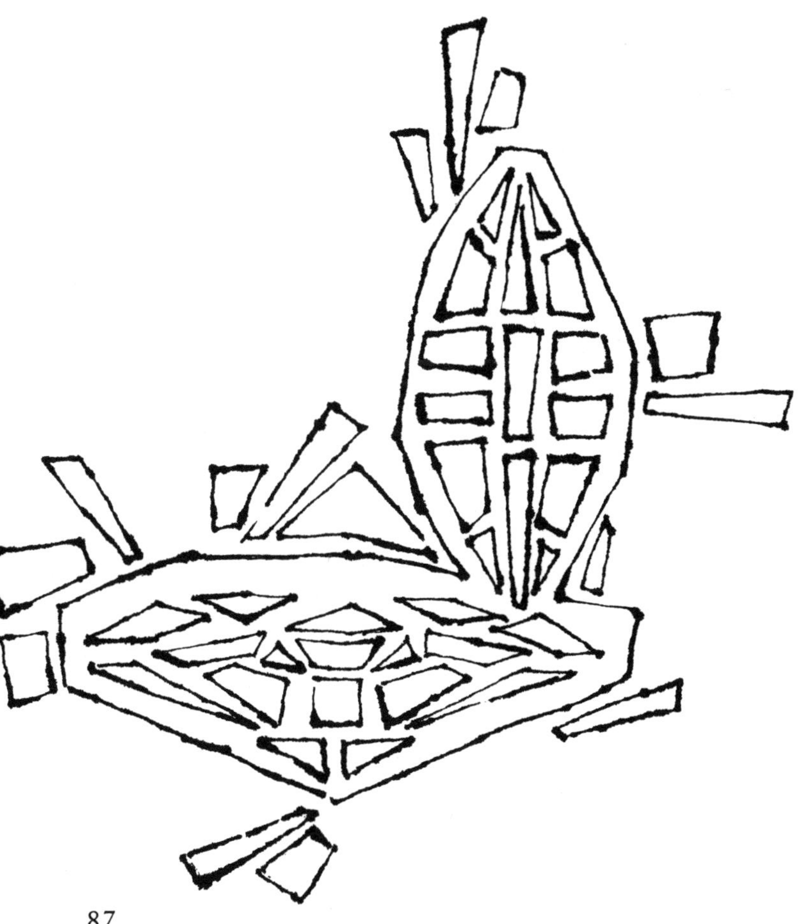

day's end

O Lord, evening is a wonderful time!
As the day wears out, I do too.
We both seem to get there at the same time.

And then darkness comes.
And quiet settles on the town.

Weary people come home, yawning and drooping.
It is time to relax, to let go, to unwind.

O Lord, I'm tired tonight too.
I didn't know just how tired
  until I sat down.
Then I all but collapsed.
Even my brain is at half-mast.

But it is evening now.
Things undone will remain undone
  until I can catch my breath,
    and, refreshed,
  can start a fresh new day.

Lord, give me restful sleep tonight.
Turn my mind off.
Restring my unstrung thoughts.
Let the peace which Christ alone can give
descend and stay with me this night.

Let me awake in the morning
clear-eyed and clear-minded,
with renewed strength
and eagerness.

But first, please Lord,
grant me rest—real rest—
and sleep!

the years on parade

The years march on, Lord, like wooden soldiers on parade, one much the same as the one before. From the spectator's point of view they all look quite uniform, trim and orderly, but almost uninteresting in their sameness.

If we could call a "parade rest" we could see the differences much more clearly. Each does have its own individuality. So Lord, let us make the most of each year as it comes. They do not have to be monotonously the same.

(All have their joys, all have their sorrows,
Be with us, Lord, through all our tomorrows.)

Keep us from making the same mistakes,
causing the same hurts to those we love,
from fighting the same battles
when the wars are over.

But we need your direction, Lord. Otherwise this year will end up with the same frustrations, the same feeling of having gone nowhere, with a sameness that just won't quit.

(All have their joys, all have their sorrows,
Be with us, Lord, through all our tomorrows.)

Make each year a new adventure,
a time for regained vigor and zest,
an opportunity for special growth,
a chance to deepen faith,
an opportunity to serve you, Lord,
as I never have before.

Yes, we pray at the sunup of a fresh New Year:
Be with us, Lord, in all our tomorrows,
and keep us ever with you.

"O God, our help in ages past,
Our hope for years to come,
Be thou our guide while troubles last,
And our eternal home!"